Put Beginning Readers on the Right Track with
ALL ABOARD READING™

The All Aboard Reading series is especially designed for beginning readers. Written by noted authors and illustrated in full color, these are books that children really want to read—books to excite their imagination,
laugh, and support their feelings. With fiction a
interest and curriculum-related, All Aboard Rea
every young reader. And with four different rea
series lets you choose which books are most app
growing abilities.

Picture Readers
Picture Readers have super-simple texts, with many nouns appearing as rebus pictures. At the end of each book are 24 flash cards—on one side is a rebus picture; on the other side is the written-out word.

Station Stop 1
Station Stop 1 books are best for children who have just begun to read. Simple words and big type make these early reading experiences more comfortable. Picture clues help children to figure out the words on the page. Lots of repetition throughout the text helps children to predict the next word or phrase—an essential step in developing word recognition.

Station Stop 2
Station Stop 2 books are written specifically for children who are reading with help. Short sentences make it easier for early readers to understand what they are reading. Simple plots and simple dialogue help children with reading comprehension.

Station Stop 3
Station Stop 3 books are perfect for children who are reading alone. With longer text and harder words, these books appeal to children who have mastered basic reading skills. More complex stories captivate children who are ready for more challenging books.

In addition to All Aboard Reading books, look for All Aboard Math Readers™ (fiction stories that teach math concepts children are learning in school); All Aboard Science Readers™ (nonfiction books that explore the most fascinating science topics in age-appropriate language); All Aboard Poetry Readers™ (funny, rhyming poems for readers of all levels); and All Aboard Mystery Readers™ (puzzling tales where children piece together evidence with the characters).

All Aboard for happy reading!

To my new baby boy, Dylan Roger Clarke,
with whom I am eager to share the wonderful
world of reading—G.L.C.

To Jan—P.M.

GROSSET & DUNLAP
Published by the Penguin Group
Penguin Group (USA) Inc., 375 Hudson Street, New York, New York 10014, U.S.A.
Penguin Group (Canada), 90 Eglinton Avenue East, Suite 700, Toronto, Ontario,
Canada M4P 2Y3 (a division of Pearson Penguin Canada Inc.)
Penguin Books Ltd, 80 Strand, London WC2R 0RL, England
Penguin Ireland, 25 St Stephen's Green, Dublin 2, Ireland
(a division of Penguin Books Ltd)
Penguin Group (Australia), 250 Camberwell Road, Camberwell, Victoria 3124, Australia
(a division of Pearson Australia Group Pty Ltd)
Penguin Books India Pvt Ltd, 11 Community Centre, Panchsheel Park,
New Delhi - 110 017, India
Penguin Group (NZ), Cnr Airborne and Rosedale Roads, Albany, Auckland 1310, New Zealand
(a division of Pearson New Zealand Ltd)
Penguin Books (South Africa) (Pty) Ltd, 24 Sturdee Avenue, Rosebank,
Johannesburg 2196, South Africa

Penguin Books Ltd, Registered Offices:
80 Strand, London WC2R 0RL, England

Library of Congress Cataloging-in-Publication Data
Clarke, Ginjer L.
Freak Out! : animals beyond your wildest imagination / by Ginjer L. Clarke;
illustrated by Pete Mueller.
p.   cm. — (All aboard science reader. Station stop 2)
ISBN 0-448-44308-2 (pbk.)
1. Animals—Juvenile literature. I. Mueller, Pete, ill. II. Title. III. Series
QL49.C59 2006
590—dc22

2005016047   10 9 8 7 6 5 4 3 2

ALL ABOARD SCIENCE READER™

FREAK OUT!

Animals Beyond Your Wildest Imagination

By Ginjer L. Clarke
Illustrated by Pete Mueller

Grosset & Dunlap

Can you imagine a whale

with a horn like a unicorn?

Or a lizard that can fly?

Some real animals are so strange

that they seem like make-believe.

But they are not.

Some of these creatures

have terrible teeth.

Some of them are super-smelly.

Some are deadly!

And all of them are odd and amazing.

Are you ready to freak out?

Chapter 1

Strangers from the Sea

What is that glowing in the deep, dark ocean?

It is a **viperfish**. The viperfish has lights around its dorsal fin and along its sides.

These are called photophores (say: FO-tuh-fors).

These lights help the viperfish see in the dark.

The viperfish uses a glowing lure

attached to its dorsal fin

like a fishing pole.

A fish is attracted to the light

and comes close.

The viperfish unhinges its jaws.

Chomp!

It traps the fish behind its fangs.

The **stonefish** is the most
poisonous fish in the sea.
Its poison spines can
even kill a person!

This bumpy, spiky fish

hides on the floor of the sea.

It looks like a rock.

When a shrimp stops to rest,

the stonefish jabs the shrimp

with its dagger-sharp spines.

Slurrrp!

The shrimp is gone in a flash.

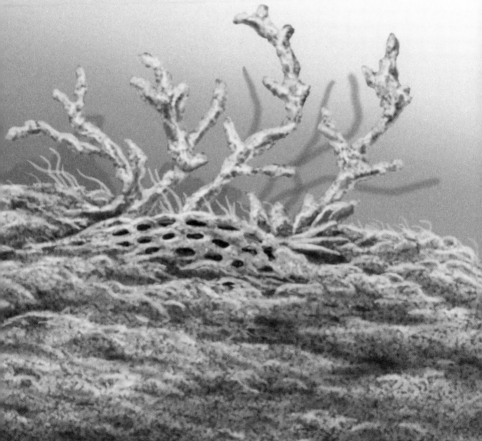

The **electric eel** is deadly, too.

And it's huge.

It can be up to eight feet long.

That's as long as a rowboat!

The shocks from an electric eel

are so powerful, a person can die

from touching one too many times.

When a fish swims by,

the electric eel sends out

strong electric shocks.

Zap!

The fish dies without the

electric eel ever touching it.

How big is a **giant squid**?

It can weigh almost one ton.

That is heavier than a polar bear!

It can be longer than 65 feet.

That's almost as long as a blue whale!

The giant squid has the

largest eyes of any animal.

They are the size of volleyballs.

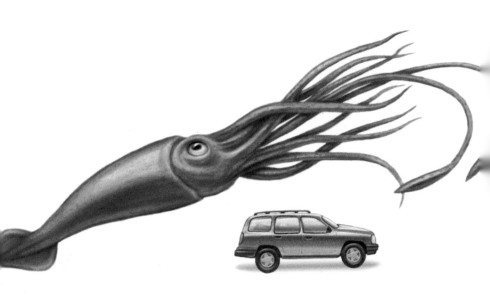

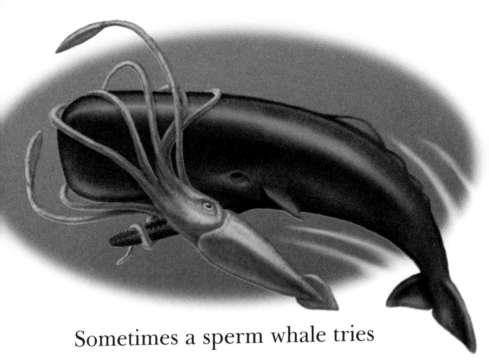

Sometimes a sperm whale tries

to eat a giant squid.

But the giant squid fights back.

It wraps its long tentacles

around the whale.

The giant squid squirts ink

to confuse the whale.

The whale is not hurt,

but it leaves the squid alone.

What a battle!

Chapter 2

Insane Insects

Stinkbugs are small,
but they have a big, bad smell!
A bird swoops in for dinner.
The stinkbug lets out a terrible odor
that warns the bird to leave it alone.
The bird flies away to find
something better to eat.

Many types of stinkbugs

eat poisonous plants

that make them taste bad,

as well as smell bad, to predators.

But that doesn't always protect the stinkbug—

people in some cultures still eat them!

Stag beetles are the wrestlers
of the bug world.
The males have huge jaws.
They don't bite, but they use
their jaws like antlers
to fight each other.

Pow!

One stag beetle grabs the other
and lifts it up into the air.
The other stag beetle acts fast.
It opens its hidden wings
and flies away.

S-s-s-s-s!

Is that a snake hissing?

No! It is a **hissing cockroach**.

This cockroach is one of the only bugs

that can make sound when it breathes.

Hissing cockroaches hiss

when they are upset.

These bugs are big, too!

They can grow up to four inches long.

That is as big as a mouse.

Some people keep these cockroaches

as pets because they are interesting,

but they sure are noisy!

The **walking stick** is the
longest bug in the world.
It can be up to one foot long.
There are many kinds of walking sticks.
Some have wings and some have spines
that look like thorns.

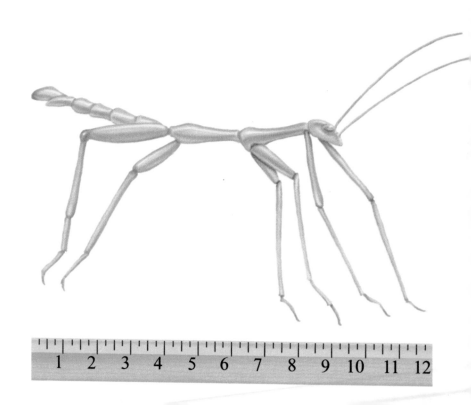

Can you spot the walking stick

hiding on this page?

It sits very still and sways a little

to move with the branch.

A bird flying by will not notice it.

This ability to blend in is called

camouflage (say: KAH-muh-flazh).

Chapter 3

Crazy Lizards

Does this lizard have two heads?

It looks like it, but not really.

Most lizards have skinny tails.

But the **stump-tailed skink** has

a round tail that looks like a head.

The skink stores fat in its

short, stumpy tail.

When this bird tries to attack

the stump-tailed skink,

it pecks at the wrong end.

The skink is not hurt because

its tail is covered in scales

to protect it from predators.

The **blue-tongued skink** is also freaky.

If it sees an enemy,

the blue-tongued skink opens its mouth

and sticks out its tongue.

This may sound funny,

but the blue-tongued skink

has a tongue as big as its head!

This big, blue tongue is so weird
that it scares other animals.
Now that is a good trick!

Have you ever seen a lizard fly?
The **flying lizard** has
stretchy flaps of skin attached
to its sides and back legs.
It uses these flaps like wings
to glide among the treetops.

Look out! Here comes a snake.

This flying lizard puffs out

its neck sac to look bigger.

The snake does not move.

Whoosh!

The flying lizard spreads

its wings and floats to a lower branch

to escape the snake.

The **frilled lizard** puts on a freaky show.
It can make itself look much bigger
than it really is.
It has colorful flaps of skin
around its neck.

When another lizard comes close,

the frilled lizard hisses and

stands up on its back legs.

It opens its frill like an umbrella.

The other lizard is scared

and runs away.

The frilled lizard goes back

to basking in the sun.

Chapter 4
Bizarre Birds

When people first heard
about the **kiwi bird**,
they thought it was made up
because it didn't seem like a bird.
The kiwi is real, but
it is very strange.

It has tiny wings and cannot fly.

Its feathers are thick like fur.

And unlike most birds,

the kiwi sleeps during the day and

hunts for insects at night.

But even though the kiwi is different,

it is still a bird.

And like other birds, it lays eggs.

This odd-looking bird is a

hoatzin (say: WAT-seen).

It is also called a "stinking pheasant"

because it can be super-smelly!

Its shiny blue face and big, red eyes

almost make it look like a lizard.

The hoatzin drops down from its nest

in the rain forest to catch a crab for dinner.

Suddenly, it sees a caiman

slinking through the water.

Caaaaw!

The hoatzin shrieks

and flaps its wings as a warning.

But the caiman does not move.

The hoatzin makes a nasty smell

like a skunk, but even worse.

Now the caiman swims away fast!

The **king vulture** has a very

colorful head.

Because it's bald, it has no

feathers to get bloody when it eats.

The king vulture is a messy eater.

It eats only dead animals and garbage.

The king vulture's hooked bill

can rip and tear flesh.

These birds usually eat in large groups.

Sometimes they eat so much

that they are too heavy to fly.

What a huge, strange bird!
The **cassowary** has a large
bony crest on its head
that it uses to dig in the dirt for food.
It has a bright red-and-blue neck
and long, fleshy flaps called wattles.
The cassowary cannot fly,
but it runs and swims fast.

It is usually shy and stays away

from people.

But it can also be very mean.

If a cassowary is cornered,

it jumps and kicks to fight back.

The cassowary has long, spiked claws.

It can rip a person's stomach open.

Or even kill a person!

Chapter 5
Amazing Mammals

The **ratel** (say: RAY-tel)

is small but fierce.

It has teeth so sharp that

it can kill a buffalo.

It will fight other dangerous animals

like snakes and scorpions,

and even larger animals and people.

Because it does so much fighting,

the ratel has thick, loose skin

to protect it, but the ratel

usually attacks first and wins.

The **giant pangolin** is built
like a tank.

It has thick, overlapping scales
all over its body.

It can be up to six feet long.

That is as tall as a person.

This pangolin senses danger.

It rears up and runs on its hind legs.

It uses its tail for balance.

The pangolin also raises its

sharp scales to make it look bigger.

If it cannot reach safety,

the pangolin curls into a ball

that is almost impossible to unroll.

All dolphins are gray, right?

Wrong!

Dolphins can be blue, white, or black.

Some are speckled or striped,

and some dolphins are pink!

Scientists have different ideas about

why these dolphins are pink.

It could be the food the dolphins eat.

But we are not sure.

Pink dolphins live in the
Amazon River in South America.
This pink dolphin is hunting for fish
in the swirling water.
Its tiny eyes cannot see well,
so it hunts by sound.
Snap!
The dolphin uses its long,
thin beak to grab the slippery fish.

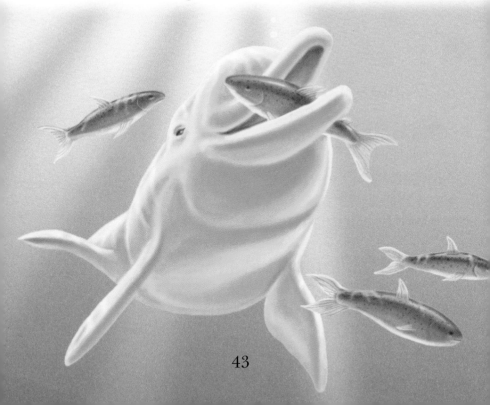

A **narwhal** looks like
a dolphin with a unicorn horn,
but it is actually a whale
with a long tusk.
The male narwhal's long, spiral tusk
grows out of its top lip.

This tusk might be used

like a sword for fighting.

Or it could be used to dig up food

at the bottom of the ocean.

No one is exactly sure.

Have you ever dreamed
of an imaginary animal?
Like a lion with horns,
and wings, and spots?
Or a flying pink dragon?

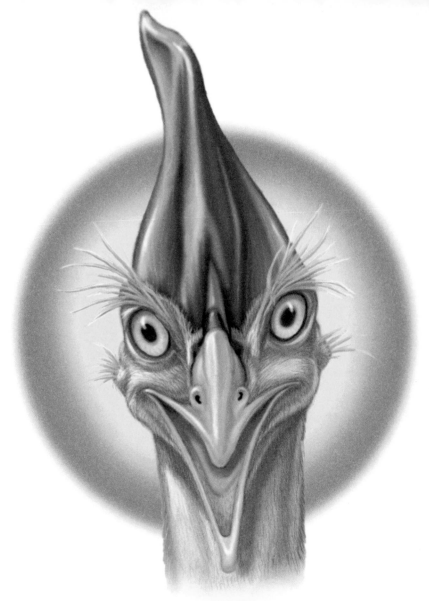

Those animals are make-believe,
but sometimes what's real
can be stranger than anything
we ever could have imagined!